"Joseph Harrison ... is entertaining because he has so brilliantly mastered the formalities of English versifying. His great gift ... is for 'play,' and it's the way Harrison plays with both form and meaning that constitutes the charm of *Someone Else's Name* ... Its presiding genius is really Shakespeare, a mentor Harrison seems almost to challenge in a sequence of twenty-two linked sonnets ... In his post-modern way, Harrison all but outbids Shakespeare ... There's a good deal going on under his fancy dress."
    —Anne Stevenson, *London Review*

"Mr. Harrison's technique never fails him, his capacity for conveying the deepest and most subtle feelings is sure and accurate. Best of all, in every poem here, irrespective of mood or weight, the reader will encounter the sheer joy of a poet gladdened by his own art, alive to the liberties and limits of form and imagination—playful, serious, gifted, multi-vocal, and athletically adroit."
    —Anthony Hecht, from the Introduction

PRAISE FOR *IDENTITY THEFT* (2008):

"Joseph Harrison's new volume is a wonderful leap in his poetic development. Harrison fuses formal control with a rich interiority and composes many poems that deserve to become canonical."
    —Harold Bloom

"How deeply satisfying it is to read a poet whose meditative, elegiac temperament is married happily to verbal wit, even laugh-out-loud humor. Joseph Harrison is that rare poet, one whose command of craft suits him equally to produce a two-line 'Ode' ('O elevated visionary thoughts, / Where are you now?') and a ten-page public poem ('To George Washington in Baltimore') on that American giant who understood the 'human scale.' A poet so giddy with wordplay that he dares to rhyme 'my palm is piloted' with 'Pontius Pilated' and 'pirated,' Harrison addresses nonetheless the most serious concerns. Wary of our technology-dominated present and future, in which 'identity theft' is no joke (and 'what fave new world is beckoning?'), Harrison makes his fingerprint evident in all of these poems—an implicit affirmation of something unique in each of us."

    —Mary Jo Salter

"The title poem of Joseph Harrison's second book is a witty and headlong discussion of how one's self, if any, is constituted. We are a patchwork, it develops, and the same might be said of Harrison's book, which makes continual and expert use of Spenser, Wordsworth, Horace, Villon, and other predecessors. If this makes *Identity Theft* seem a three-ring circus, the important point is that Harrison is a superlative ringmaster: his book throughout is governed by that playfulness and performance which, as Frost said, are required in poetry however impassioned or serious. I found myself particularly moved by 'Who They Were,' which recalls the poet's mother and father in the stanza of Tennyson's 'In Memoriam.'"

    —Richard Wilbur

PRAISE FOR *SHAKESPEARE'S HORSE* (2015):

"Joseph Harrison's poetry is modern without being modernist. That is, he employs the tools and materials of traditional poetry to construct a kind of verse that is appealingly new, yet never transgressively so. His poems reflect a renewed lustre in our direction, and we come away deeply refreshed."

    —John Ashbery

"*Shakespeare's Horse* is Joseph Harrison's full emergence as his own poet, still in the eloquent and formal tradition of Richard Wilbur and Anthony Hecht but with an accent now pitched in a new mode. Among the book's triumphs are 'Wakefield,' the wonderful 'Dr. Johnson Rolls Down a Hill,' 'Damon,' and 'Harrison's Clock.' Yet I take a particular joy in the brief but enigmatic 'Hamlet' and the remarkable title sonnet.

"The kind of comedy that Harrison works into his subtle meditations is refreshingly original. Should he further refine his already agile art, there will be no one in his American generation who so challenges the eye and the ear to come together."

—Harold Bloom

THE IMPOSITION OF ASHES

THE IMPOSITION OF ASHES

ASHES

EARLY POEMS

JOSEPH HARRISON

Syllabic Press

BALTIMORE, MARYLAND

ISBN-13: 978-0692793213

Library of Congress Control Number: 2016917164
Syllabic Press, Towson, MD

Syllabic Press
200 E. Joppa Road, Suite L-101
Towson, MD 21286
syllabicpress@gmail.com

CONTENTS

FOREWORD

Robert Schreur

In his famous letter acknowledging receipt of *Leaves of Grass,*
Emerson remarked, with some puzzlement, that there must
have been "a long foreground somewhere" to have made such a
first book possible. Very few readers would have had a similar
response back in the late 1980s to Joseph Harrison's first book,
The Imposition of Ashes—primarily because the book was un-
published then and almost no one got to see the poems. I was
one of the lucky few. And I was puzzled.

We met as graduate students in the English depart-
ment at Johns Hopkins. Coming from the Midwest, I was
prepared to be intimidated by nearly everything and every-
one. Joe was older than I, obviously better educated, obviously
more gifted. Adding to this, his sure Southern decorum made
my insecure pretensions nearly debilitating. To my great for-
tune, his graciousness easily overcame these.

Much of my bafflement was the product of typical grad-
uate-student ignorance about poetry. Still, there was valid
reason to wonder at the time, who was this poet, and who did
he think he was, so overtly turning changes on later Auden,
later Stevens, later Frost, and even Spenser himself, even if it
was early Spenser? The long foreground of these poems was
not only the poet's own past but also quite conspicuously,
and audaciously, his knowledge of the poetic past extend-
ing through to Virgil and Theocritus. What to make of this?
And, more critically, what had the poet himself been able to
make of this?

Definitely some of this literary high-mindedness was a
young poet's untested and as-yet-unrealized ambition. But
it's striking now, reading the book some thirty years later,
how achieved and truly beautiful much of this poetry already

is. Perhaps Harrison the poet did not fully know what he was up to, or up against, in these poems, but his muse certainly did. A glance at his later work confirms this. The ensuing accomplishments retroactively justify and enliven the earlier work, proving that what had seemed like it might be inspiration in his first book absolutely was. It's clear now that only a muse who could foresee "Air Larry" and "Shakespeare's Horse" could have given a beginning poet lines like "Imagining's the thing's the thing" and "Out of the carnival dusk full of shadows and echoes."

Reading *The Imposition of Ashes* after the fact of the later, published books, is a remarkable experience. Rather than finding in this first book a Whitmanian torch shining back into the shadowy foreground of an ever-receding past, there seems to be a revolving searchlight here that both illuminates the future work and reflects back from it to reveal sights previously hidden. Passages and strategies in *Someone Else's Name* and *Identity Theft* which had been dark and difficult to discern now spring into view. Brilliancies in *Shakespeare's Horse* now shed light on enigmas in this first book, explaining some and showing that others are in fact genuine enigmas and not mere uncertainties. It's as if an under-drawing revealed by x-ray did not merely show an artist's preliminary efforts but made clear intentions that otherwise would have remained invisible in a long-admired painting. And that masterpiece in turn now seemed to welcome the unveiling of a previously unknown and otherwise lost work of genius.

In *The Imposition of Ashes* it is sometimes an open question whether the poet can live both with and up to what is imposed on him. And, given the burden of his sometimes almost uncanny self-consciousness, it also can seem an open question whether he has ultimately imposed these obligations on himself and so is imposing them on his reader. Might his poems in fact too facilely show "Fold upon fold of fabrication," as he fears in "Bartram's Trail"? Do his forms provide him not "unusual freedom" but only cells for an imprisoning "containment"? Could he be just the slave of a tradition he cannot master, a "drudge of the field's persistence"? These concerns continue and deepen in the later books, but what may have seemed like open questions in the first book can now be seen to have been firmly rhetorical ones, generative of the remarkable rhetoric that follows. While *The Imposition of Ashes* is not itself a canonically great book, its publication now shows it to stand among the "vividest" ones.

Emerson greeted Whitman at the beginning of a great career. Being able to read Joseph Harrison's first book after the accomplishments of his subsequent work is like finding yourself newly greeted by a poet you had thought you already knew. You find yourself confirmed in the always-new vitality of poetry. There is indeed the "flick" here that Wallace Stevens described, like "some first thing coming into Northern trees" which "Adds to them the whole vocabulary of the South."

THE IMPOSITION OF ASHES

I

Gulliver, persuaded from early childhood escape
Kept you propped above your private stage and window
Shifting the patchwork landscape like a quilt, woke up.

The quilt was gone. It was damp under the trees.
The urge to peer in beech hollows persisted,
Beset by strictures of a warning voice.
Then, bending around the vine-encircled trunks,
Fingering the fallen oak, the scattered cones,
Sun lit the stagnant water, a stale mist rose
To linger at the cleft of the beech like words,
Old and of utmost pertinence to him.

He blanketed the forest with intention.
The pines, the ashes, and the dark magnolias
Pointed down the trail to the local marvel:
A crystal creek with beaches of white sand
Studded with trove on trove of clustered stone.
And were their blues and roses, their slate, their quartz
Arranged to spell a name, his name to come?
Heady with revelation, he wandered off
With some new sense of what old path to follow.

So Gulliver discovered he had never
Left either the magic window or the forest.
Waking, he was still dazzled by the ridges,
By hidden valleys and twin peaks like knees.
And if the casement opened too easily on
Fold upon fold of fabrication, those insect
Minutes after noon, when the forest gathers
Itself and starts to hum, when even the vines

Relax, and crafty, foraging, out early,
The genius hereabouts, the wizened coon,
Scuttles invisible in the underbrush,
Remained for him the vividest book, always.

GULLIVER IN THE WHITMAN
NATIONAL FOREST

He slept beneath the mountain's face,
Dreaming of pure cold printless still
White fields set high in star-carved space,
Destined for shoes his feet would fill.

He dreamt the ghosts kept silent, gone
Like elk tracks lost in snow and glare
Or buried campsites of charred stone,
Then dreamt he heard them line the air

In voices layering his mind,
Syllables sticking on his tongue,
Impedimenta stiff as wind.
A white lament, pure echo, hung

Above the whistling, barren scene's
Banked terraces of ice and snow
Blank with a brilliant, blinding sheen.
The "yes" he hoped for froze to "no."

Was every tale a tale of frost
Till only rime remained for him?
Each storied dream-pool iced across,
Sheer blades to drink, sure death to swim?

One day of sun melts little ice
Where glaciers are the ancient rule,
Where water, cold in cost of place
Yet free enough to drip and pool,

Can make one day a day of spring
If only in a single drink.
"Imagining's the thing's the thing,"
He thought in waking on the bank.

He leaned down to the water, drank,
Saw rivers freezing on his face,
Arched out over the mirror, sank
Into himself—without a trace?

FARER

On the next day I woke and saw
The ruined beach, the surf's rough claw
Dragged back across the shore's silt scars,
A scene fixed by malicious stars.

The sea had cast me up again.
Echoing through icy rain
The screaming of strange circling birds
Riddled the world and made it weird.

The day blew colder. The surf ceased.
The waves creaked in thick chains of ice.
Resurfacing in chronic care
I walked that beach and read tracked there,

Scrawled in sea-wrack, the rime-cold score:
The shore recedes yet stays the shore.

7

SONG FOR VOICES

"In the Beginning was Scar,
A Tearing of All,
The Tear of a Star.
Light is its own perpetual Fall"—

"Renewing our sight!
No wound blessed the first bone.
Light is falling not fallen, light, light,
On leaf and stone."

DIRECTIONAL

In the ashes of the sacred fire pit
A dirty towel lies crumpled. The mound
For offerings has fallen, kicked to crumbles,
And now a million willows stand neglected,
The medicine waiting, patient in the bark.
The spirit lights vanish "no more forever"
Across a continent sown with arrowheads.

There were people here before we were
Who worshipped rocks and streams and trees
As their dead rolled round with the earth
To return in the steam
Of water sizzling on the giant coals,
Alive in the chattering of the stones
And the gyrations of mysterious lights.
They lay praying in the vision pit three nights
And, chanting, danced for days in the sun
Till all directions folded into one.

This ancestral landscape haunted them.
And does something still inhabit the meadow's garden,
Among the leaves and the voices of the birds,
Almost audible in the voices of the birds,
    Silently calling *O my descendants, O my relations?*

Are the dancers stirring under the hill?

2

We all crawl into the dark
Of the canvas hut, willow-spined.
"When you enter this place
You enter another time,
A place of no time
And all time.
The old people have been
Crawling in here
For two thousand years."

And the rocks are thrust in,
Tunkayatakapaka,
Furious little furnaces
Breaking with light, a low, red light
That smells like earth itself.
Then, sweet with the scent of the prairies,
Sage crackles on the rocks,
The shaman screeches,
The water splashes and hisses
And you gasp
As the steam kicks deep in your lungs.
And the lights start flashing.

3

"O You, winged Power from the place where the sun goes down,
You with the ancient and sacred guards,
And You, winged Power living where the Giant lodges,
From whence come the strong and purifying winds,
And You, from the place where the red sun rises,
Guardian of the light and giver of knowledge,
And You, Controller of the sacred winds,
Living where we always face, giving life with your breath,
From whom and to whom our generations come and go,
And You, Spotted Eagle, circler in the highest heavens,
Seer of all things in the heavens and on the earth,
And You, beneath us all, Grandmother and Mother,
Ancient, sacred earth from whom our bodies come,
And you also, all of you, winged peoples of the world,
Kingfisher and meadowlark, blackbird and woodpecker,
Snowbird, crow, and magpie, hawk and dove,
Eagle hawk and bald eagle, you are all included,
There is a pinch of tobacco here for each,
Sealed with tallow in the sacred pipe.
Help us, help us, we are crying for a vision!"

4

Help me, help me with this lamentation:
A whole world, a whole people lost,
Given no way out as themselves but to die.

Our generous freedom slides on,
Its great iron wheels greased by virtual genocide. . . .

5

Lemuel took four onions from the top
Of the refrigerator. He rolled them
On the table top, rolled them around
Until they held the corners of the room
Tight to the ground. He marked them in
Polarity, imagining one white, one green,
One rolling off the edge and one
Illumined by a momentary star.

"Two of these orbs are firm as North
And South, and when I palm them
The foundations steady. Yet one
I have almost forgotten, and one
I must, in sorrow, live and breathe,
Lying split open at the western door,
Blurring these lines, biting my throat,
Glazing this room as in a wash of tears."

6

When I went back
To the little farm in Glenelg,
Years later, the little white shaman,
His long hair now gray,
His face puckered,
Looked at me funny:
"What made you come back?"

I don't know.
I didn't go back
To sit in ceremonious dark
Unable to believe any more,
To hear the stones chirping,
To see the lights sparking,
And not think the timeless
Dead returning, only
"He's sure got his tricks on tonight."
Perhaps I just wanted to sharpen
A few tricks of my own.
Or perhaps I simply wanted
To hear, just once more,
The old story:

"This was my vision:
I knew they were planning
To develop this land,
I had seen the surveyor
Again that morning, so I
Went up to the top of the hill

To pray for this land,
And I was crying and praying,
'Grandfather, *Tunkashila*,
Save this land
And I'll live here the old way,
Let me keep it your land,'
And I saw an eagle in the east,
And it turned and dove toward me
And as it passed it brushed
My left cheek with its left wing,
Then it turned in the west and dove
And as it passed it brushed
My right cheek with its right wing,
Then I turned around
And there at the edge
Of the woods was a man
Dressed like a hobo or clown,
And I was embarrassed
Because he could see me crying,
But he smiled
And as he started to walk away
He turned into a badger.
So I called Turkey
To ask what it all meant,
And he said that I'd licked 'em
And would never see that slick
Surveyor again, and I didn't."

But I knew that story.
I didn't go back for that.

7

So I came away from what I could not bear
To carry off and plant like a flag and proclaim
Or press inside other leaves or number or name,
Knowing I had no place to stand by that culture's bier
Reading my spirit's trace in an eagle's flight.
What I had thought might be power was only desire,
No tongue can translate the undersong of that fire,
The colors of paint obscure the colors of light.

VANYSSHYNGE

"And forth she wente, and made a vanysshynge"
— CHAUCER

But if I tried to give you form from earth,
Dark furrows thick with sleep, seeded and stilled,
You'd dream the thin green fingers' crawl to light.

Or if I tried to whirl you to a cloud
Fanned by my breath, brief curlings of a face,
You'd dream the warm harmonic fall to earth.

Or if I tried to channel you to runnel
Framed by my ribs, you'd press against the frame,
Shape me to hold a deeper roll of water.

And so your love of change prevents my love
From any figure but a plummeting stone,
Cooling projection of your vanished star,

Or I can never find you in the fire
Where these clay hands shrink hissing back to bone
And jets of flame extinguish even stone.

II

.

WOMAN WRITING

She does not seem
To pose, but sees
The painter, sees
You, and smiles in
Immediate
Love, as if, though
You interrupt,
She wanted to
Stop for you, to
Stay there, patient,
Full with your child
Forever. The
Viewer does not
Think of her as
Eternally
Burdened, constrained
In each close breath,
Her private love
Drying like paint
(Soft folds of white
Fringed with yellow),
But believes her
Happy, though she
Can never turn
Her eyes away
To write again
Till you release
Her eyes from yours,
Which you never
Will, Jan Vermeer.

MARYANNA

The line clicks dead. What good, in the end, is regret?
Each word is weighed and weighted, sometime, next time. . . .

But as another summer surrenders its promise
The question turns urgent, the air stiffens,

Laced with the implications of departure.
All colors wilt in the redundant heat.

It would be cooler in the dim cathedral
Where she may be waiting, silently asking

For you to come and ask her what she wants.
Who can help her in her human sorrow?

That wine is sour, that wafer is hard as stone.
The pews stir in the half-light. The restless dead

Murmur their hymns of hurt, their selfish fears,
Their disappointment. Him and her, her and him.

MONDAY MATINS

It may be that somewhere Penelope still waits,
Attending the light. She is never quite alone,
But she can tell from the slant of the sky
That something's wrong. That speck on the rim of her world—
Is it a sail? And is it coming home, or going away?

Down goes the night with its patient, faithful
Unraveling of our story. Up comes the day.
That web you are caught in, Penelope,
Is it of your weaving? Or does the angling sunlight
Fix you to seal you in waiting, making you stay,
Leaving you brushed to a figure of patience?

COMPLINES

Will they ever get on the same track,
What you want to be and what you are?
The days are discarded, turn by turn.
The moon comes up again and you are the same.

Only far under the bark, in the deep rings,
Change has been quietly working. Only now
Do you see it, only now you don't want it.

When I come back to the room where I was a child
More comes back than me. The "big red fox" grins
And the shelves are alive. The books about sports
And animals straighten up and sit ready.
Husks of old selves, dry as the moths in the light
Under which the child played and played in his trance,
Crumple in silence as I cross the room.

Will we come to a truce, if not peace?

The children played in the shadow of the rock.
Their shadows swam in the shadows of the trees.

This summer the rock, cleared of ivy, stood
High as my knee. It's hard to imagine
How it dwarfed me then, or remember
The little yard as a long course, the running,
The calling, the fireflies momentary stars
Dotting the ever vaguer motions of those evenings
All gone into a world of light turned dark,
Evenings when the games rushed on two hours
After supper, and summer was a giant in every shadow. . . .

The trees knew as they let the moonlight through
And threw the shadow of the rock far down the lawn,
The rock that was our base, our home, safe at home
For the present, firm under the sloping night,
As every night the mother still remembers
The echoes of a thousand summer evenings
And the children's voices race the darkened lawn.
Their shadows swim in the shadows of the trees.

Some things come back at night without their shape,
Featureless old friends, games without rules.
I'm asleep, of course, and stir lightly in sleep,
Not knowing what summer I'm in, or what vague pleasure
Keeps me returning, each day, to someone's house.

It's like remembering the music from a movie
You saw as a child. You never knew its name,
And slept through most of it, and missed the plot.
But one scene keeps returning with its music,
A scene on a terrace, or in a garden,
With two people quietly talking, two or three.
Someone was saying something about pleasure
Becoming sadness, though it's not quite what
They said that you remember, but the vibration
In their voice as they said it, and the way
The others nodded. You did too.

And I wake almost knowing what I dreamed:
The game I made up, the new neighbor I befriended.
I played with both all summer. Summer ended.

III

FAT TUESDAY

Out of the carnival dusk full of shadows and echoes,
Over wrought-iron petals, under pocked brick arches,
Around shotgun and camelback and skinny-shanked stick houses,
Through the private corner of the secluded courtyard,
Where the trellis net crawls at lengthening angles
On the half-erased sundial and chipped, mildewed angels,
Up out of the flat earth veiled and defined
By palmetto and magnolia, by borders of crepe myrtle
And wisps and scarves of the drowsy, ubiquitous moss,
Up through street cries, wheels, hooves, the whole musical
      shuffle,
Out of all this it rises, a crimson stain up the late winter sky,
As if at the pivotal hour of the dormant year
The dust rose flowered, filmed shape and petaline gesture
Dissolved in confusion, something alive in the vines,
And the past kisses the present one more time,
The river slides through theaters of chronic festival,

And something keeps pushing up through the hats and the cloaks,
Something keeps bubbling in the pralines and the prawns,
Something keeps thudding deep in the bottom strings
And sweeps like a vagrant smile across the torchlit zoo of masks,
And everyone stops what they're doing to go outside
Among businessmen and students and roustabouts
And generations of their ancestors and descendants
Fanning out from this day like the spokes of a giant wheel
As the river spreads its fingers over the plain,
Turning in concert around a single figure
Dancing alone, a man dressed like Walt Whitman
Dancing and chanting one word, over and over,
And no one can hear that word, but they all breathe it in

And murmur in echo of its single, rich syllable
A word beneath the word, a sound like the sound of the sea
As it calls and rises and gathers all revelry in
Out of the carnival dust full of shadows and echoes.

THE IMPOSITION OF ASHES

I

Ahead of you someone is waiting somewhere,
Idling, stretched on the grass, breathing
An air he wants you to breathe for a little while.

But why should you eat of his offering?
Why accept all things and sides as filtered from him?
He will impose himself on you if you are not careful.

2

Not that he hasn't been imposed on in turn
By whatever has made him the child of the grass
Pushing up through him insisting on itself,

Sweet grass and velvet grass and the cool zoysia,
Chocolate brown sleepy grass and squirreltail,
Quackgrass and spiked goat grass and foxtail barley,

The slough-grass dangling wand-shaped pannicles,
The silver hairgrass like diminutive hemlocks,
Zizania and poverty oatgrass and Job's tears.

Assured of his return to what he plunders
He reaches down into the mulch of names
Compressed like the pages of a book,

Stuttering, mimicking, beginning to recite.

3

"These are only ashes but you have to bear them . . ."
To whom were these words directed as you
Sat reading? Whose brow was crossed?

Who sensed their own indictment as if chiseled
In obscure letters over a gate that writhed
With figures wrestled in its hardening iron?

There's no one here to hold your hand if you enter
Or lead you forward like a friend and master
Deciphering the lamentations as they rise.

4

Not that there isn't someone walking beside you
Or a silent step behind you to your left
Whose shadow you can see at certain moments

When the road swerves like another one you've been on
In a dream's landscape or something you once read.
That bridge you've seen, that field, that single tree.

But can you hold him responsible for the markings
You find scribbled on the stones that line the way,
Indicators of direction and metrical distance

That examined closely become the embellished
Illuminated initials of flowering lineage
Graven within the hills and the dust in the rock?

5

Ask him this question directly
And he will evade you. But turn back
To surprise him as he creeps behind you

(Not when you see his shadow—he's not there then)
And seize him as he freezes,
Pale as if apprehended in a crime,

Then he will start to tremble, and let fall
What he elaborately fails to conceal:
Two tears the size of white grapes, pendant, cool.

(Travelers before you have sipped that poison,
Wanderers before you have drunk that honey
And seen the water starting from the rock.)

He will prove a hairless, shrunken creature,
A once-winged being reduced to a stick figure
Or disquieting caricature of a human

By the withering landscape he has tracked you through,
Persuaded that you carry close to your body
The only sort of nourishment that can save him.

6

But why struggle from one crossroads to the next?
Why submit to the course's ardor and compulsion?
Why wrestle with something always slipping undone?

The flutter of guilt in your voice when you say,
"I have to admit I don't read poetry,"
Why does it even arise this late afternoon?

Of course you could always close it and turn away.
You could simply, puzzled, return it to the shelf.
The story is that you opened it at all.

7

A tree falls in the forest. No one hears
But the executioner who has labored at it,
And the birds who have lived in it, and the curious squirrels,

And the old trees who tense their roots against the crash,
And the young ones who now can push into the light,
And the moss and lichens that will bury it.

But mainly the axman hears, and takes his pleasure
From the great oak's giving way and his own exhaustion,
And for a moment that pleasure is enough.

8

To relinquish that epic dream of completion and answering,
To banish the native desire for something larger,
To turn in the midst of the festival alone,

To break free of that inaccessible referent
And liberate its pronoun to be yourself,
Whomever you address as close as close . . .

9

It was then your life swung into view behind you,
Or what passed for your life, the story of it
That you told yourself as you slipped along.

Do you remember when it was you first began,
Waking in shadow on a bed of flowers,
Narcissus, hyacinth, and eglantine?

Or, following the murmuring of water,
The day you found the glassy liquid plain,
A perfect mirror, holding the whole sky?

Should we have stayed there forever, you and I?

10

But you don't remember that original scene
Any more than the warning voice that called you away
To betray you to your twin and brother.

And now when you look into the bathroom mirror
You start at seeing something so substantial.
The moment is never purely specular:

His features, carriage, and odd nervous frown
Betray the fear that a third person's watching.
You always look "to see what others see,"

And could wander years in search of your reflection
Yet never find a surface deep enough
To cast you back beyond community.

If that first motive still remains it's been diluted,
Till now the single thing you want to see
Is your image catch fire in their reflecting eyes.

11

Or perhaps you turn up elsewhere in the story,
As the body that wants to be whittled
To voice lifted by wind,

The body that once was only voice,
Soft whistle of the wind parting the grass
Before the birds called from the apple trees,

And as pure voice had the freedom to meander
Among the other voices, the ones with bodies,
Adopting a particular tone or cry,

Flitting on to absorb another, favorite color
(As a bee samples the sweets of a field of flowers
Not knowing he's the drudge of the field's persistence),

Skirting the deadly awkwardness of silence,
Never having to speak first in conversation,
Never cueless and panicked, laboring for breath,

And always reserving the power of truncation,
Selective in redoubling to the others
Their words inflected with your fragmentation.

If once innocent of this in your love of beauty
You soon grew conscious of your mediation
And felt your wings sag toward a hardening body.

12

But turn back to when your life in this form
Began, seven winters ago, that Christmas
You came home as if for the first time.

Is it impossible to recover the pristine
Wonder of those moments, when you felt yourself
Swelling and beginning to stammer out

Your sense of the great journey you were starting?
It swept forward as if driven by another
Whose style propelled your loose mnemonic hand

Through long syntactic curves and languid pauses,
The limpid phrases strung like cirrus clouds
Across a salmon-colored western sky,

Which seemed in its accumulate formations
The map of whatever country you were in,
A treacherous one, showing roads not yet built

And blooming in the place of what it charted
As the light began to die and the clouds unfurled
And the land beneath shone like soft yellow parchment.

And you some freedom had in this, peaking
On another journey to exotic fields, pausing
To drink from a mountain stream on the way to Tibet,

As, purling, clean, the first clear word shot out: "Gulliver. . . ."

13

Those days inspiration was luck and literal fire,
The sequestered hour in the house alone,
The stolen bud unfolding to the match.

Twenty, thirty minutes arced above
The monotonous gray medium of the day
Then dropped back down as you put down the pen.

And the rain came again, evasive, ungenerous,
Imposing itself on a field of expectation
But thinly, stingily, not raining much,

As you straggled forward lured by the illusion
Of profit without long labor, the lightning stroke
That made flagrant expenditure worthwhile,

Eater of ashes and eaten by them,
Until even that rise and fall lost its seduction
And the viewless sun stepped behind the Olympics,

And the last tiny, pocketed flame snuffed itself dark,
And the final puddle wiggled into the ground.
Then hardly a word from her for what seemed like years.

And the gift/curse, buried, put forth roots.

14

Meanwhile that other life congealed around you,
The one with people in it, and food, and love,
And news that lit the room and glazed its panes.

It was time to grow up, to go back to school
And start never learning everything again,
To take your temporary incomplete

And stretch it till its elasticity
Opened spaces all the way to the horizon
In the folders and cabinets deployed around the room,

Into which the sheets and slabs of paper fell
Like layers of a geological map,
Showing where you had been, and with whom, and for how long.

And from under that mountain of interest and obligation
One late winter day a single page slid loose,
As a stream wiggles out between snow-covered rocks.

15

The festival starts again, and the canvas breathes.
The ground quickens close to the figures it focuses.
Discs of color form and begin to rise

Against the brickwork and the ironwork
Which seem to inhale as if they could set aside
Their architectural posture for a day

And move as the festival moves, as the plumes of the dust
Arch and crumble and are swept up again
By the breath of the wind or its attendant ghost.

The hands on the clock in the foyer know it and like it,
The napkin rings nudge each other drowsily as it curls among
    them,
The moss feels its dear attention and sags with love.

16

And if the mumblings of a hundred separate tongues
Mingle in confusion to resemble a chant,
Thudding, insistent, dumb, song without words,

Who is the hub around whom the carnival spins,
Whose sonorous voice, sweeping but never final,
The disembodied breath of what crucified son?

Or what is the axle that turns him like a knob?
What crux only tightens as he wriggles against it?
What pattern folds him back into the grave of rock?

17

The persistent absence of the simplest word
Traces his song as it's written in reverse,
Becoming something else in spite of him,

A scalded cry the machinery of centuries processes,
Interpreting, codifying, printing, distributing,
Making available for ritual recitation

By the man and woman and child in the street
Able to relax there only on this day
And half a dozen other days a year.

The figures filing past as the scene winds down
—The fat man in the hat, the round woman, their slender child—
Give me a vaguely accusatory look as they trudge back inside

And the economy of the carnival gleams like nails:
These forms, which seem to offer unusual freedom,
Are only given me for my containment.

And so I knelt for the imposition of ashes,
Knowing little about Catholicism
And its terrible calendrical precision,

Raised Presbyterian, and that not far,
But drawn (by something in my culture's childhood?)
To imagine an order this child never knew:

Led by nuns to the church in its half-light,
The smell of candles burning, the solemn,
Familiar priest, the smell of the ashes themselves,

Dust of last year's palms in a little cross,
The blackened thumb, the pressure of the mark,
The pulsing of the priest's low metronome,

Black ash on whitened ash, ashes on dust.
I came to these signs claiming no right to them
To find they claim to have a right to me.

Give me the strength, O moon, to convert this moment.

19

As I turned and spoke to myself for the last time:

You were never the placid victim, always Barrabas,
Never the word gutted in sacrifice,
Always two-tongued, conceitful, and now free,

Though retaining from your imprisonment
An impression of the other prisoners' faces.
And if that apparently pure one's image

Reproduces itself at mechanical intervals
On the fluent surface of your expression,
You were more literally marked by the lament

Of the blind man muttering in his doubled dark,
Old author of insurrection and of murder
Praying he might slaughter enemies once more:

"Forgive them not, they know not what they do."

20

Thus marked and sent forth
Into a land of light and little water
I have come out of that land a little early

To scan its formations from the nape of the pass.
West the plain levels toward the city.
I don't know how long I will be suspended between these
    contraries

But I know the stages of the journey
Like the chromatic progression of the leaves:
Daybreak's forest, yellow for parting at noon, memory's
    brown.

And if I never knew whether the monuments
Preserved in their lapidary signatures
Something besides themselves the far side of sound

(The crux is the point of erosion on the monument's face,
Not just the whorls made by the wind
But fingerprints and all acts of disfiguration),

By these leaves put forth for my sustenance
In the desert I knew myself sentenced
To rehearse three trials Adam never knew:

The difference between his names and the green world,
An other really other, not just rib,
A childhood he had lost or almost found.

21

Then Anticlea came, whom Tiresias beat off.

51

22

These are only ashes but you have to bear them,
To carry them from one crossroads to the next
And even unto your crucifixion and even beyond,

Though they will come to seem alien and repellant
As eventually your sense of them will resemble
That of a person who is otherwise dead

And can see but not quite read the movement of his words
As it mimics that of shadows cast by fire
In a dark place far from the light of the sun.

23

But to mention the sun is to dream of that world again,
To dream that one might live again there as well,
If only in making the grass grow for a few seasons,

But to be rising again and stretching our fingers,
To surface as a blur in the season's color
Or curl against the feet of those who follow . . .

And a further dream, that the red lights float
Staining the sea with a god's death,
That from his death might come food, and wine,

That the light has descended into the cave
To bury the spring's explosion deep in the hillside
So that the vines burst and crackle and the flowers ignite.

24

He woke. The curved heavens
Hurled themselves wheeling forward
As he read the paths of the planets

Hurtling through time
As the light of the stars hurtles through space
And the particles of the light whirl and spin

And an infinitesimal light-ringed particle might whirl.

25

There was a suite of rooms in front
With paintings of landscapes and cases of artifacts,
Then a room with a statue of a woman looking away,

Then a hallway with a few old photographs,
Then you turned the corner into a large room
And were surprised at the spaciousness and light,

The walls crowded with scenes from scripture,
At one end of the room a cross, on the opposite wall a painted cross
(There's no one on it) catches fire and as you focus on it

Crumples.
          Brush the ashes off your clothes with this.

26

He rode into the city a day early
But could imagine the palms and the pressing crowd
And his reluctance to be transfigured, his desire

To snap back what he said like a whip,
But one never can as it spirals off
Attracting the commentary it prefigures,

Orbiting in relation to other planets
(Occasionally an alignment of these provides the shield
Behind which a new one forms at the crest of time),

Only here space is curved so wickedly
The bodies in motion shoot whistling across the sky
To arc in flares against the figured stars.

27

And you who have tracked this through the flowering cave
A step or two behind it to its left?
It thinks, it knows you're there, though it is blind

To your approaching shadow as it falls.
Half lost in light, a figure turns a final time.
He has the sustenance you desire, the bright, immortal fruit.

He will give it to you, yes, but you must return it.

28

So you stand at the point of reversal, ready to reascend,
The only thing down here with a chance to escape.
Turned back upside down, is the predicament the same?

It doesn't involve an equation of perceptions:
What to you has seemed kaleidoscopic flight
Has looked all black and white from the inside.

And from the inside your eyes are all that's visible
In the moment they reflect and distort the inscription,
As if you were the only way back to life.

But you're tired. My pronouns are weakening at last.
Yet just look at all the reference we've established,
You and I and the you that was me and is now gone,

The he from whom I've always been estranged,
And the almost finished series of small abstracts.
But in the end you are the missing _____.

Please take something with you when you go,
If only a vanishing memory of the grass
Covering the continent in sweeps and folds,

Witchgrass and weeping lovegrass and smooth chloris,
Vanilla grass, silver-beard, and spartinas,
Toothache grass, hilaria, creeping panic,

Quaking grass, cheat, bull muhly, banner sorghum,
The water-whorl grass swaying in pond shallows,
And the everlasting and the nimble will and the maiden cane
      parting

Comes forth a child, smiling and holding out his hands.

30

Now I can finally say to you: Come,
These things are neither fully mine nor yours,
Yet taste them and repeat their measure.

THURSDAY AT 8:00

after the rustling into place among the chairs, and the awk-
wardly over-descriptive introduction, it starts and all try to
concentrate, though some drift off and others in and out and
others on, liking the voice of it and an occasional image, a
sparrow flicked across the windshield's lens and vanished
into the rain and snow and storm outside, but even if the
brevity of this vision almost seems to figure life itself, this
is no reason for conversion, especially not the one desired,
of the event into something that brushes our landscape at
evening, coloring the perceptions of the people in it, and
now even the consoling fiction that saying it is so makes
it so, that the room is not really quiet but quietly humming
with people breathing in rhythm with the words, which taste
like wine on the lips, like bread on the tongue, cannot be
sustained, and this failure is the wellspring of lament, the
origin of the furious flowers on the margin, brilliant against
oblivion, and of the paranoiac shadow of vaulting ambition,
self-propelled on elaborate, flimsy wings, and plummeting
as the pitcher begins to sweat and someone falls asleep and
the reader grows suspicious of the same old lines, beginning
to wish for some unusual protection, like a barbed wire fence,
between him and the blurring faces that absorb him without
expression, much less the dreaded and desired stare of accu-
sation that would at least give him an accomplice, guilty in
the recognition of guilt, as he thinks to himself, "Not one of
you will deny, not one betray me tonight again and again."

ARIEL AND MIRANDA TO EACH OTHER

ARIEL

Take the clear reflected sky
    Imprisoned in this glass
I live to hold, not caring why
    The way you, turning, pass
Across its glance gives its old lie
    Some of your graceful ease.

MIRANDA

    But does that please
You who can never body yourself forth
        Except to trace
The curves of others' hair and limbs and mouth,
    And so displaced
Must make a single figure do for both?

ARIEL

And do it does, in seasons when
    Cotton floats fill the pool's
Reflection, earth shoots green again
    From sempiternal cools,
You lift your hat in the warm rain,
    Forget the six months' rule.

MIRANDA

    But ruled, my friend,
You'll never by your own volition be,
        Swirling to blend
Worldly clay and vitreous fantasy,
        Until we end,
Sifted in the metamorphic sea.

ARIEL

Or metaphoric, as we rise
    Elaborate and strange,
Emerald bones and garnet eyes,
    Figures of slipping change
Coloring like the eastern sky's
    Cumulus mountain range.

MIRANDA

    But of the pain
You suffer as your airy coloring
    Covers the plain
Old truth that you, poor fool, can barely sing,
    You don't complain,
And yet that lacking your dumb love's nothing.

ARIEL

Love's nothing, yes, and never love
    But never found or known
Except as that which lovers move
    To lie against a stone,
Blind to the sidereal show above
    Once the old riddle's gone.

MIRANDA

    You riddle, sly,
Persistent spright, determined not to leave,
    Not knowing why
When the last hands lie still you cannot grieve,
    But only cry,
"Revise, revise, deceive, deceive, deceive!"

As if there were no cost
To being what we are,
Nothing spent or lost
In managing the air,
The fire-ringed portal crossed,
And safely landed here

We could contrive another show,
Familiar folk in a strange land,
With you what's left of Prospero
And I of creature Caliban
As through the whirling words we go,
Ethereal hand in earthly hand.

ECLOGUE

ARGUMENT: *Thenot, a distinguished old shepherd-scholar, and Cuddie, a rude, ambitious young shepherd-poet, debate the relative merits of their crafts, which argument is adjudicated by Hobbinol, who proposes a singing contest between the two.*

THENOT.

How sweetly pleasant our idyllic life!
Ivory gleams in the sun; the young folk call
And laugh and rush about us; we amble on,
Vested in robes of wise seniority.
I came across an interesting fact today
Which I noted and shall shepherd with great care:
Walt Whitman once wrote, "Spenser was E. K.!"
Now what do you suppose gave rise to that
Curious fantasy? It's certainly
Material for an article or note.
That coed on the grass has ample breasts.

CUDDIE.

How you disgust me with your pedantry!
The poet nicks his image from plain wood:
He has no use for the academy,
For crusty canons and stale hierarchy,
But touches that core element in us all
Of what we feel with sad bewilderment,
Stroking the ancient chords of love and time.
He will enrage the people to pull down
This tower, and raise another in its place,
Its opposite, no crumbling, claustrophobic
Stairs, no Gothic spires, no hallowed lists

Of hollow tomes, no strangling ivy hair.
See how her thin skirt limns her shapely ass.

HOBBINOL.

Cuddie, rude boy, best placate old Thenot.
Don't be so quick to haughty condemnation
While you're still eager to accept your check.
Besides, dry dogs may dig up useful bones.
The two of you should chat in harmony:
His mild obliviousness is no threat
Unless you trigger dormant jealousy.
And don't project some sprawling audience
You'll never have and wouldn't know what to do with.
The institute as forum is a fact
You'll never get outside of. (Colin claims
Otherwise, and will play outlaw—let him try.)
Meanwhile you two shall have a singing contest
For the favor of that beauty you both fancy.
Keep the syntax simple. Old goat, you first.

THENOT.

Now when I lay green and easy under the apple trees. . . .

CUDDIE.

Flaming edge of night flying
Stars guttering in their sockets
Eyes like suns upon us blinding us
Wandering blind and lost weeping
The lost company among ruins
Forlorn and solitary uncomprehending
The violently erased inscriptions
Dying ignorant of the flaming letters

Setting us alight like stars
Falling from above screaming afire

(CUDDIE rushes off in flames as THENOT metamorphoses into a bench.)

HOBBINOL.

And what brings Colin to the quad today?
Shouldn't you be at home, pacing and fretting
About some line in your perpetual book,
Or plotting your canonical self-inscription?
I have my criticisms, as you know,
Of what I've seen: it's still too literary,
Too wrapped in its allusions, too entranced
With all it knows and wants to say at once.
It doesn't always seem entirely human.
The personal touches—those are what I like,
The places where a palpable life shows through.
But several things disturb me, most of all
The bad faith of the whole Christian thematic.
What right have you to that if you don't mean it?

COLIN.

Every, none. It's virtually accidental
If carefully planned. The sacred warps into
The secular, transposed to be redeemed—
Or does its alphabet of stubborn bones
Glow with recalcitrant significance?
And what redemption lies in this cracked ploy:
Turning the sentient nocturnal sky
Around old axes of self-reference?
That thus dissolved ritual dissipates,

67

Water splashes the altar rather than blood,
No sacrifice occurs, just the mad act
Of trudging forth to petty stings and snares,
Death being something other than such play?
Or does an older order start to creep
Up from the rich mulch of the figural dark,
Revealing codified calendrical signs
As ancient impositions on natural time,
Equinox, solstice, ecliptics of the moon?
But then is this growing stain shadow or wound?

HOBBINOL.

I won't deny that you're quite clever, Colin,
But grants and laurels take institutional time.
You have to apply, you have to apply again.
Aim for professional security
Before attempting half you comprehend.
Meanwhile please try to cover the connection
Between your intertextual machinations
And the dull yeoman's work you have me do.
As for the canon, you're one of the six hundred.
The regnant creed is careful understatement.
What is the point of bold transumptive moves
When the whole game may soon be rendered over,
Even the famous manner of life after death?
But if you intend to ride this front and center
Please release me from your service soon.

COLIN.

Hobbin, I write your lines, we both know well.

HOBBINOL.

And what are we writing now, a villanelle?

COLIN.

An eclogue, one that swerves to culminate
In an elegy that almost ends my book,
Or would if I could show it without shame.
The story of its composition's strange.
Once when I was writing nothing at all
A fearful whisper struck my dumbness down:
The poet my father was dying. Just as in
The last pale seconds before sunrise Venus
Glares like a dawning star, I saw him gem
The eastern morning sky then disappear.
I felt the silver water well, loosened
By the hoof of the dying stag, and knew
My hour had come to wrap him in my song.

The rumor of his death was only that.
Self-horrified, I looked at what I'd done,
Eager to save the murmur of lament
That kept my tongue from turning back to stone.
So now I tune a song that can't be sung,
Without that song my book is never done.

HOBBINOL.

O careful Colin, this is not your theme,
However you admit your guiltiness.
Sing rather your complaint for Rosalind
When she spurned your continual suit again
And left these bleak fields for a distant land.

COLIN.

When you came back from the hospital
Summer was fading
And you were fretted with fever,
Your friend was dying, your friend
Was dying,
Your beautiful, gentle friend.
All day you shrank from hideous images,
The loved one turned a death's head.
At night your dreams were the beating wings of doves.

The leaves catch fire and tumble in the wind.
The birds catch fire and plummet like the leaves.
The crippled remnants of the season cry
For sudden frost to numb their lingering.
At another time the larkspur will return,
Scarlet and yellow columbine will flourish
And slender thalia hang its silken bells
In open woods, the dwarf wild rose will flare
And blue wisteria climb the colored air,
But never will this young man rise again
To greet the parting friend with open arms.

This is the leaden fact we cannot lift,
The dull crux where we can say nothing more
Than what's proved ineffectual before.
In another's loss we weep our own,
Sprinkle flowers, scratch a name in stone,
Pretend our ceremonies are a gift
To the failed body we will not let drift
Into the dirt and roots and underlife
But wrap in a container like a jail.

Don't go, we say, don't go, be something still
Beneath it all, a spot we can revisit
Like the thought of a single moment years ago
And there you are, your limbs restrung, your face
Rinsed clear by light, moving in light, with light.

Weep shepherds, then weep more.

HOBBINOL.

Here is no cosset Colin,
Yours be your own reward.

(Exeunt Hobbinol.)

COLIN.

Now I have something to explain:
I made this from another's pain.
I did not love your friend who died
But when you cried
I held my cup out in the rain
And caught your grief so I could write again
(For the truest art is the most feigned),
Even if I lied:

Lay it to rest, release the subtle breath
That filled the quiet corners of this room.
Lay it to rest, its master's left its home.
It used to hover in our expectation,
Never quite arriving, always departing,
Brushing the live air. But it is gone.

It is gone with you, sweet friend, who were so
Hospitable, embracing all who came
To stay near you and murmur your clear name:

A tree, its fruit. When next to the woods we go
Nothing will seem to link the trees together.
The upstate graves will vanish under snow.

Out of high night an errant star descends
To flare a while, then slowly cool to stone.

This is as sad a thing as we have known.

As I entered the cave its floor was moist underfoot, & its walls were soft clay, & it echoed of falling water, & could I have seen the walls I might have seen legends of hunting pictured there, but that chamber was dark or I was blind in that place

Then I entered a second chamber where the floor was cool like marble, & it was filled with columns like chrysolite, & it echoed of lamentation, & in that soft light I saw it was ringed with people, & that a woman of inarticulable love-liness was staring at me with inhuman steadiness, but approaching her I realized she was just a painted figure, & that all the people were painted in that place

Then I found myself in a vast third chamber, on the ledge of a cliff-face, & heard the sound of water crashing on rock, & the mist was on my face, & from my forehead shot a beam like the light from a projector in a theater, casting images of those I loved onto the chamber's opposite wall, & the expressions of my family & friends seemed to change from love to admonition then back, & then to sorrow, & I cried out & stepped toward them into the mist

And down into a fourth chamber, where the high ceiling was domed & gilded, & echoed with the beating of wings, & the walls were adamantine, & marked as if licked by fire, but there was no lamentation audible, there were no prisoners there, & in the center of the chamber stood a stone tablet which read

Forty days he shall wander without human kindness
Forty nights he shall lie on inhospitable rock
He shall find no water but after long searching
He shall find just enough food to keep him alive

then what seemed an angel stood before me, his mouth &
eyes arched in a perpetual *"no,"* & as I tried to pass he seized
me & we fell grappling, & through no strength but that of
feinting did I wrestle free

To wake bruised & weary in another chamber, which was
filled with dust, & the smell of decaying parchment, & the
sound of mumbling, & I could not see for the dust, & could
not breathe, & could not hear myself think for the listless,
perpetual mumbling, & a heavier sleep than any I had known
came over me, & my material journey ended there

Though I dreamed I woke again in a sixth chamber, where
the walls & floor were of a white substance I did not know, &
which was open at the top to the light of the sun, & though
I was too tired to climb out, there was some peace in staying
there, & in the middle of the chamber was an elaborately
whittled cage, & in the cage were nineteen songbirds, white
with black markings, & I let the birds go

ENVOI

Little book submit to those
Who will say what they choose.
You have everything to lose
Only to those readers, though few,
Who know to read you through
They must read through you.

Thirty years ago I put together a book I called *The Imposi-
tion of Ashes*, made up of poems I wrote between 1980 and
1987, when I was still in my twenties. It was a sprawling
thing, more than twice as long as this version. I had copies
made at a copy shop and gave them to my friends. I offered
the manuscript for actual publication: there were no takers.
A magazine published one of the poems. Eventually even I
lost interest in it.

One person I gave a copy to was Robert Schreur. When
he asked, nearly thirty years on, if I had ever revised the book,
I admitted I had, mainly by throwing much of it out. The
poems I had kept I kept essentially as they were, in form and
in intent, where these could be discerned. I made occasional
repairs to phrasing where I could. But changes more ambi-
tious than these seemed neither possible nor wise.

It is difficult for me, now, to relate to who I was then, as
a poet (and as a person). I wouldn't conceive of poems in this
way, or go about writing them in this manner. I will confess
a slight unease in seeing them in print at all, unsettling my
gratitude to Robert for wanting to print them, and my plea-
sure, which I don't deny, at seeing them finally in page proofs
after all these years.

I do not send them forth now, to what public I may
have, as the statement they originally intended to be, having
long since lost confidence in their imagined merits. Nor do
I expect scholars of my work, were there ever to be any, to
scrutinize them for signs of promise. Nor do I offer them
as implicit advice to the young, a kind of cautionary tale
suggesting that their notions about what poems do are likely
to change as they mature: the ones who need to be told this
will find out soon enough, on their own.

But I would not be who I am as a writer, I believe, without the young man who wrote these poems having been who he was. I owe him a certain debt, however puzzled I find myself by his ambitions, and his rather oblivious fearlessness, and despite my shudders, here and there, at moments when his reach exceeds his grasp. However far we have been fortunate enough to come, our earlier selves can only encourage humility, and here the debt I owe him is repaid, for what it is worth.

Joseph Harrison
NOVEMBER 2016, BALTIMORE

Joseph Harrison was born in Richmond, Virginia, grew up in Virginia and Alabama, and studied at Yale and Johns Hopkins. His book *Someone Else's Name* was named one of five poetry books of the year by *The Washington Post* and was a finalist for the Poets' Prize. In 2005 Mr. Harrison received an Academy Award in Literature from the American Academy of Arts and Letters. He was awarded a Guggenheim Fellowship in poetry in 2009.

Mr. Harrison's poems have appeared in *The Antioch Review, Arion, Birmingham Poetry Review, Boston Review, Center, The Common, The Hopkins Review, The Kenyon Review, Measure, The Missouri Review, The New Criterion, The New York Review of Books, nuovi argomenti, The Paris Review, Parnassus, Poetry Northwest, Raritan, River Styx, The Sewanee Review, Sewanee Theological Review, Smartish Pace, Southern Humanities Review, Southwest Review, unsplendid, Western Humanities Review, The Yale Review,* and elsewhere, and have been featured on Poetry Daily and Poets.org. They have been anthologized in *The Best American Poetry 1998* (ed. John Hollander), *180 More Extraordinary Poems for Every Day* (ed. Billy Collins), The Library of America's *American Religious Poems* (ed. Harold Bloom), Penguin's *Poetry: A Pocket Anthology* (ed. R. S. Gwynn), Penguin's *Literature: A Pocket Anthology* (ed. R. S. Gwynn), *The Swallow Anthology of New American Poets* (ed. David Yezzi), and *Leadership: Essential Writings of Our Greatest Thinkers* (ed. Elizabeth D. Samet).

Joseph Harrison now serves as Senior American Editor for The Waywiser Press. He lives in Baltimore, Maryland, with his wife, Carla Harrison.

OTHER BOOKS OF POETRY BY JOSEPH HARRISON

Shakespeare's Horse (The Waywiser Press, 2015)

Identity Theft (The Waywiser Press, 2008)

Someone Else's Name (The Waywiser Press, 2003; Zoo Press 2004)

The Fly in the Ointment (1994; 20th Anniversary Edition, Syllabic Press, 2014)

OTHER BOOKS BY JOSEPH HARRISON

Editor, *The Hecht Prize Anthology 2005–2009* (The Waywiser Press, 2011)

Editor, with Damiano Abeni, *Un mondo che non può essere migliore: Poesie scelte di John Ashbery, 1956–2007* (Luca Sossella Editore, 2008); translated by Damiano Abeni and Moria Egan, with an introduction by Joseph Harrison

www.ingramcontent.com/pod-product-compliance
Lightning Source LLC
LaVergne TN
LVHW091228080426
835509LV00009B/1208